OUR SOLAR SYSTEM (SUN, MOONS & PLANETS): SECOND GRADE SCIENCE SERIES

The Solar System comprises the sun and everything that orbits around it, including planets, moons, asteroids, comets and meteoroids.

The Sun is the
star at the
centre of our
solar system.
The Sun gives
life to the Earth.
The sun is 150
million km away
from the Earth.

Mercury is
the smallest
and closest
to the Sun.
Mercury has
no atmosphere
which means
there is no wind
or weather.

Venus is a terrestrial planet and is sometimes called Earth's sister planet because of their similar size. Venus is sometimes called the morning or evening star.

Earth is the only astronomical object known to accommodate life. Earth is often called the ocean planet. Its surface is 70 percent water.

Mars is often referred to as the Red Planet. Mars has many massive volcanoes.

Jupiter is the largest planet in the Solar System. Jupiter is the stormiest planet in the Solar System.

Saturn is the least dense planet in our Solar System. It is most famous for its beautiful giant rings.

Uranus was the first planet discovered by telescope. Uranus turns on its axis once every 17 hours, 14 minutes.

Neptune is the
farthest planet
from the Sun.
Neptune is the
most dense
among the
giant planets.

Moon is Earth's only natural satellite. It is one of the largest natural satellites in the Solar System.

Titan is the largest moon of Saturn. It is the only moon in the solar system with clouds and a dense, planet-like atmosphere.

Callisto is a
moon of the
planet Jupiter.
Callisto is
composed of
approximately
equal amounts
of rock
and ices.

Io is the
innermost
of the four
Galilean moons
of the planet
Jupiter. It has
the highest
density of all
the moons.

Ganymede is
the largest
moon of Jupiter
and in the
Solar System.
It is the only
satellite in the
solar system
to have a
magnetosphere.